Annemarie van Haeringen was born in the Netherlands. She is a Dutch illustrator and picture book author and illustrator. She studied art at the Rietveld Academy in Amsterdam. Annemarie has illustrated numerous children's books, worked on a series of films, and created illustrations for several children's magazines.

She won the Golden Brush Award three times—in 1999, 2000, and 2005—and a silver award for *Coco and the Little Black Dress* in 2014. This is her second book with NorthSouth.

Text and illustrations copyright © 2015 by Annemarie van Haeringen.
First published in Holland by Leopold under the title *De Parkiet, de Meermin, en de Slak*.
The parakeet, the mermaid and the snail is the property of the Stedelijk Museum Amsterdam.
English translation copyright © 2016 by NorthSouth Books, Inc., New York 10016.
Translated by Jan Michael.

First published in the United States, Great Britain, Canada, Australia, and New Zealand in 2016 by NorthSouth Books, Inc., an imprint of NordSüd Verlag AG, CH-8005 Zürich, Switzerland.

Distributed in the United States by NorthSouth Books, Inc., New York 10016.
Library of Congress Cataloging-in-Publication Data is available.
ISBN: 978-0-7358-4263-2 (trade edition)
1 3 5 7 9 • 10 8 6 4 2
Printed in China by Leo Paper Products Ltd., Heshan, Guangdong, April 2016.
www.northsouth.com

MIX
Paper from responsible sources
FSC® C020056
www.fsc.org

Annemarie van Haeringen

MR. MATISSE
AND HIS
CUTOUTS

North
South

Mr. Matisse was an artist.
He had the sun in his tummy,
and his colors made everyone joyful.

He painted with gusto: pure bright colors on high, wide canvases.

But one day the sun left his tummy.
Mr. Matisse was in so much pain
that he couldn't even sit up properly.

He went to the hospital and had a major operation.

When he woke up, he was in a white room.

"There's no color in here. You'd think I was dead.

What a nightmare!

Fetch my brushes! Fetch my paints!"

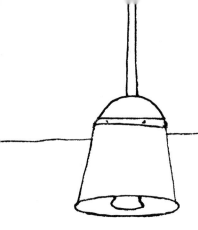

But the sheets weren't smooth and taut like canvas,

and the walls and ceiling were far away.

"Fetch my fishing rod!"

But the rod was too heavy, especially with the stitches in his tummy.

Then Mr. Matisse spotted a pair of scissors . . .

... and a bag of croissants that his assistant had brought.
He emptied the bag and cut a swallow out of it.
"Pin it to the wall, over that stain!"

His assistant brought piles of paper in all Matisse's
favorite colors.
"Excellent! Now I can draw and paint at the same time!"

When he got home, Mr. Matisse kept cutting.

He cut and cut and cut, all the memories from his travels:

the plants, the flowers, the algae and seaweed, the sponges,

the birds, and the women.

All through the night he cut.

He couldn't sleep, and he wouldn't take a sleeping pill.

"I might lose all the beautiful images if I did."

Mr. Matisse's room was his whole world, and he
was coloring it himself.

His assistant pinned the cutouts to the wall.

"A bit to the left. And that one to the right,

at an angle . . . a bit higher. That's it.

Put the snail on the right, over the radiator.

That one's too low. . . ."

The hours pass, the days, the months.

Whoosh!

"What fool left the window open?"

The woman Mr. Matisse was cutting out was blown from his hand in a whirlwind of images.

The woman swirled to the floor along with the other cutouts. She looks just like a mermaid. "Lovely. I'll leave her like that."

Fine Tahitian tissue paper landed on his lap.

He cut it into beautiful algae.

Mr. Matisse's assistant climbed up and down the ladder, contorting like an acrobat, pinning the cutouts to the wall while he played and played with forms and colors until he was satisfied.

"I'm creating directly with color.

It's what I've been striving for all my life!

Hmm, there's one cutout too many. The snail.

That'll have to go.

I'm the snail, and this bed is my house.

All that I need is around me here.

"I've made myself a garden to live in,
a whole new life."
And, like a snail, Mr. Matisse slowly crawled through his oasis.

HENRI ÉMILE BENOÎT MATISSE

(1869-1954) was born in Le Cateau-Cambrésis, France. He was a painter, sculptor, draftsman, and printmaker known for his bold use of color and form.

Matisse first began painting at age twenty when his mother brought him art supplies to entertain him as he recovered from appendicitis. He later reported that it was "a kind of paradise" and that he had decided at that point to become an artist.

Matisse became well known for his colorful paintings and sculpture until once again physical illness intervened. In 1941, at age seventy-two, Matisse was diagnosed with abdominal cancer. Following surgery in which he nearly died, he was bedridden for three months. After his recovery, Matisse turned once again to experimentation with paper and scissors. With the help of assistants he created cut-paper collages. His works started out small but were eventually turned into murals the size of rooms. He had created a new art form that combined elements of painting and sculpture.

Matisse later moved to Venice, where he created his first major cutout project for a book he put together called *Jazz,* and went on to create striking and enormous murals such as *Oceania the Sky* and *Oceania the Sea.* Today Matisse is thought to be one of the leading innovators in modern art and the best colorist of the twentieth century.